T is for Time

Written by Marie and Roland Smith
Illustrated by Renée Graef

Sleeping Bear Press
315 E. Eisenhower Parkway, Suite 200
Ann Arbor, MI 48108
www.sleepingbearpress.com

Printed and bound in the United States.

10 9 8 7 6 5 4 3 2 1

Library of Congress Cataloging-in-Publication Data

Smith, Marie, 1951- author.
T is for time / written by Marie and Roland Smith ; illustrated by Renée Graef.
pages cm
Audience: 6-10.
ISBN 978-1-58536-512-8
1. Time—Juvenile literature. 2. English language—Alphabet—Juvenile literature.
3. Time—Juvenile poetry. 4. Nursery rhymes. I. Smith, Roland, 1951– author.
II. Graef, Renée, illustrator. III. Title.
QB209.5.S65 2015
529'.2—dc23   2014026953

A is for our adorable Alessia

Love, Ahna and Gramps

☼

For Bruce

Renée

A

a

A is for Almanac.
This old book helps decide
when the season is right
for planting crops outside.

An almanac is a yearly publication. Some almanacs predict for the coming year the movements of the sun, moon, and planets, and the times of each sunrise and sunset. They give us a daily schedule of the oceans' high and low tides. Helpful information is included for farmers about the weather and the best time to plant seeds and harvest crops.

Almanacs have been used since humans first looked up and started studying the changing sky. The earliest almanac found was written on clay tablets over 3,500 years ago. One of the most popular almanacs today is *The Old Farmer's Almanac*, which was first written in 1792.

A is also for Astronomy, which is the study of the stars, planets, and universe.

Before people had clocks in their homes or wore wristwatches, bells were used to communicate time. At first, bells were small and handheld. Eventually, towers were built for big bells high on top of churches and over town squares. All the villagers and anyone in surrounding areas could hear them. Ringing bells let everyone know the time to go to bed, the time to get up, the time to eat, and the time to go to church.

Big Ben was the nickname given to the huge bell of the Great Westminster Clock in London. The bell weighs over 13 tons. It rang for the first time on July 11, 1859. The famous clock has a face on each of its four sides that shows the time. The clock tower is over 315 feet high. It is the largest four-faced chiming clock in the world. Today Big Ben is used as a nickname for the bell, clock, and tower.

B is for Bells
ringing through towns,
announcing the hours,
listen for the sounds.

A calendar is one way of keeping track of large amounts of time including days, weeks, months, and years. We are familiar with calendars that are displayed on a wall and have a page for each month divided into squares for each day. But calendars from long ago looked very different.

Thousands of years ago, prehistoric hunters carved lines on sticks and bones. Scientists believe these may have been simple lunar calendars. A lunar calendar is based on the time between moons. The lines on the bones and sticks might have been used for showing the times for hunting and animal migration or for knowing when to prepare for the first snowfall.

Early Egyptians used a calendar based on the sun called a solar calendar. It was used for thousands of years. The Romans liked the idea of a solar calendar and used it to make their own calendar. It became known as the Julian calendar. In 1582, improvements were made to the Julian calendar, and the name changed to the Gregorian calendar. This is the calendar most of the world has used for over 400 years.

C is for Calendar,
    a year on display.
On a wall or desk—
    the month, week, and day.

A huge stone structure called Stonehenge is located near Salisbury, England. It is 3,500 years old, and no one knows why it was built. Many people believe that Stonehenge might have been a calendar because its stones line up with the sun and moon at different times throughout the year.

C c

D is for Daylight Saving.
A good way to remember
spring forward, fall back
in March and November.

Daylight saving time was created to help save
energy by adding an extra hour of daylight to
the evening. Daylight saving time in the United
States begins on the second Sunday in March.
Clocks are set ahead one hour at exactly 2:00
a.m. standard time, changing the time to 3:00
a.m. daylight saving time. On the first Sunday
in November, clocks are set back one hour at
exactly 2:00 a.m. daylight saving time, which
then becomes 1:00 a.m. standard time.

Dd

E is for Einstein,
a scientist with a notion,
after thinking long and hard
about the law of motion.

EINSTEIN

Ee

Nobel Prize–winner Albert Einstein was born in Germany on March 14, 1879. At age 17 he went to the Polytechnic Institute in Switzerland, where he planned to become a teacher. After he graduated, Einstein could not find a job as a teacher, so instead he started working in the Swiss patent office.

While at the patent office Einstein wrote some of his papers about his theory of relativity. He believed that movement causes time to slow down. Albert Einstein taught at Princeton University and became a United States citizen in 1940.

In 1971 scientists tried to prove Einstein's theory. They put atomic clocks on jets, one going east and one going west, and flew them around the world. When the jets landed, one of the clocks had lost a small amount of time, while the other clock had gained a small amount of time. This proved that Einstein's theory of relativity was correct.

The part of a clock that shows the time is called the face or dial.

Clocks built in thirteenth-century Europe did not have a face. They were made to ring bells so people could *hear* the time. In the fourteenth century, clockmakers and inventors realized that the same gears that made the bells ring could be used so people could *see* the time.

Carvings in the shape of a pointing hand were made to show the hour. Unlike our clocks today, the hand did not move. Instead, a clock face with numbers slowly turned underneath the pointing hand. Eventually, clockmakers made the pointing hand circle around a stationary clock face or dial.

A clock face or dial has the number 12 at the top. The hands on a clock's face move to the right. This is called clockwise.

Ff

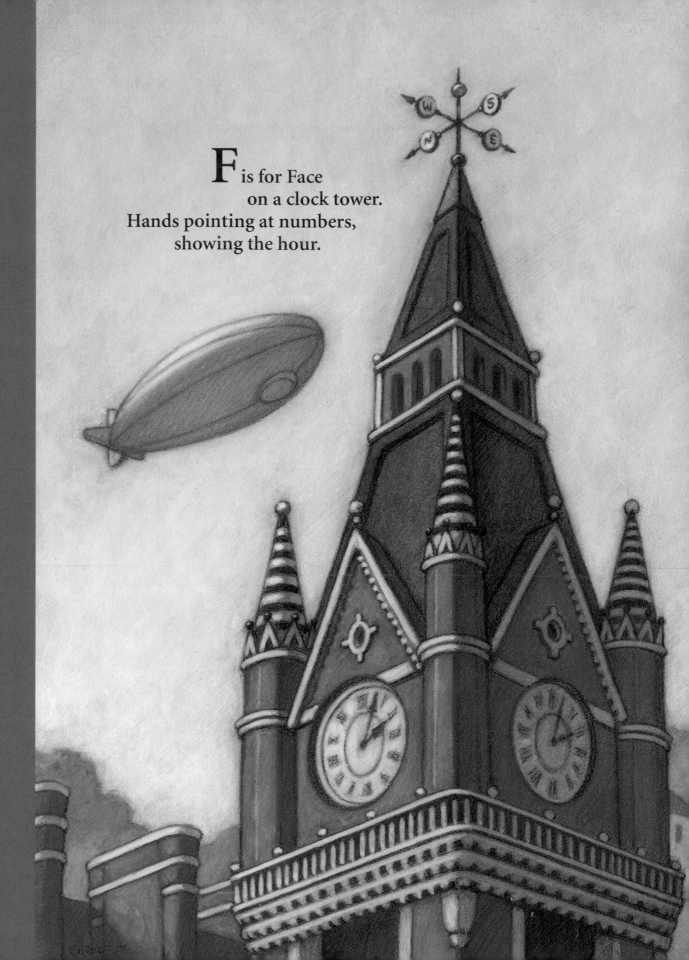

F is for Face
on a clock tower.
Hands pointing at numbers,
showing the hour.

Lines of longitude are used to measure time and distance. There are 360 lines drawn on maps of the earth that go through the North and South Poles. The first line of longitude is located in Greenwich, England, called the *prime meridian* or 0 degrees longitude. Longitude lines measure time and distance east or west of the prime meridian.

In the past, many countries considered their own city or their own observatory as the prime meridian (see **O** is for Observatory). This made travel between countries confusing. King Charles II of England started the Royal Observatory, located in Greenwich, England, in 1675. The observatory became known for its accurate maps of the world, the moon, stars, and planets used for navigation. Soon ship captains from many countries were using Greenwich as the prime meridian for longitude.

In 1884, the International Meridian World Conference was held in Washington, D.C. The people at this conference decided to make Greenwich the official prime meridian for longitude for all countries.

G is for Greenwich,
a good place to start.
Mark here a zero
on a map or a chart.

H is for Hourglass.
    Watch the sand flow
from the upper chamber
        to the one below.

An hourglass is also called a sandglass or sand clock. It is made out of glass with a top and bottom of equal sizes with a narrow opening in the middle. The hourglass is filled with a measured amount of sand. The sand flows from the top of the hourglass through the narrow opening into the bottom part of the hourglass. A person can measure the passage of time by how long it takes for all the sand to make its way into the bottom of the hourglass. Then when you want to tell the time again, you just flip the hourglass upside down.

It isn't exactly known when hourglasses were invented, but they were used on ships as early as AD 1300. Aboard ships, hourglasses were hung from hooks. The swaying of the ship did not interfere with the flow of the sand.

H is also for horology, the study and measurement of time. A person who studies time is called a horologist.

H
h

is for the International Date Line,
important while on a ship
for knowing the exact date
at the end of an ocean trip.

In September of 1522, explorer Ferdinand Magellan's crew returned to Spain and became the first people to sail around the world. The trip took three years and one month. The crew carefully kept track of every day of the historic trip. They were shocked when they realized they had arrived a day later than the recorded date in the ship's log. This created such a sensation that a special committee investigated the news and reported it to the pope.

A line was drawn on maps and called the international date line to prevent confusion about the date when sailing around the world. It zigzags around countries in the Pacific Ocean at 180 degrees longitude—halfway around the world from the prime meridian in Greenwich, England. If someone is traveling *west* of the international date line, the date is one day ahead of the prime meridian date. If traveling *east* of the line, the date is the same day as the prime meridian. Today this line is used not only by ships but also for air travel.

J j

John Harrison was born in England in 1693. When he was a young boy he learned to be a carpenter but was more interested in clocks. After teaching himself, he built a clock completely out of wood when he was 20 years old.

Early sailors did not have a way to pinpoint their position in the ocean. Because of this, ships often became lost. Sometimes they crashed into rocks, losing lives and cargo. Sailors needed an accurate clock to keep track of time at 0 degrees longitude, to find their correct position at sea. In 1714, the British government offered a reward worth millions of dollars to anyone who came up with a way to calculate longitude. John Harrison thought he could build a clock to help sailors.

Over a period of 20 years John Harrison built five versions of a clock that kept accurate time at sea. When he was 83 years old, he was finally awarded the prize money for discovering a solution to the problem of longitude. All sailors during his time, and now many years later, are grateful that he never gave up on this lifelong ambition.

J is for John Harrison,
   who received recognition
for solving the longitude problem—
   a lifelong ambition.

K is for Kukulcan Pyramid.
It has an unusual feature.
Twice each year appears
a slithering snakelike creature.

K k

The equator is the imaginary line around the middle of the earth between the northern and southern hemispheres. Twice a year, in March and September, the sun shines directly over the equator. When this happens, both day and night last an equal number of hours. This is called an equinox.

The pyramid of Kukulcan is located in Mexico. It is 79 feet tall (or about 8 stories high). Each of the four sides has 91 steps. If you add together all the steps and the platform on top, they total 365—one step for every day in a year. Scientists think the temple might have been used as a large calendar.

On the days of the equinoxes the shadow of a huge feathered serpent, or snake, seems to be slithering down the steps. The shadow is caused by the position of the sun in the sky.

The pyramid was named after the Mayan god Kukulcan.

Before anyone had an easy way to check how accurate their own clocks were, people would go to observatories to ask for the exact time. They would then reset their clocks and timepieces to the correct time. The astronomers at the Royal Observatory in Greenwich grew tired of this constant line of time seekers.

Astronomer John Henry Belville worked at the observatory. In the 1830s, he began "selling" and delivering accurate time in person using a pocket watch nicknamed "the Arnold."

Eventually it became his daughter Ruth's job to care for "the Arnold" and deliver the correct time. Ruth sold time until 1940. After Ruth's death at age 89, the family watch was left to the Clockmakers' Museum and library in London.

L 1

L is for a Lady,
while in her youth,
learned to sell time—
her first name was Ruth.

The Clockmakers' Museum has the oldest collection of clocks and watches in the world. This is just one of many clock museums around the world. The National Watch and Clock Museum located in Columbia, Pennsylvania, is the largest in North America.

A month is based on the moon's orbit around the earth, called the lunar cycle. It takes 29 days, 12 hours, and 44 seconds to complete.

Our yearly calendar is based on the earth's movement around the sun. This takes 365 days, plus 5 hours, 49 minutes, and 12 seconds. The extra hours, minutes, and seconds may not seem important, but over the years they make a difference of many days. These extra days caused many problems when using the calendar. To correct this, every four years we add a day in February, giving it 29 days instead of the 28 it usually has. And that year is 366 days long instead of 365 days. The extra day is called a leap day and the special year is called a leap year.

September has 30 days, along with April, June, and November. The remaining months have 31 days.

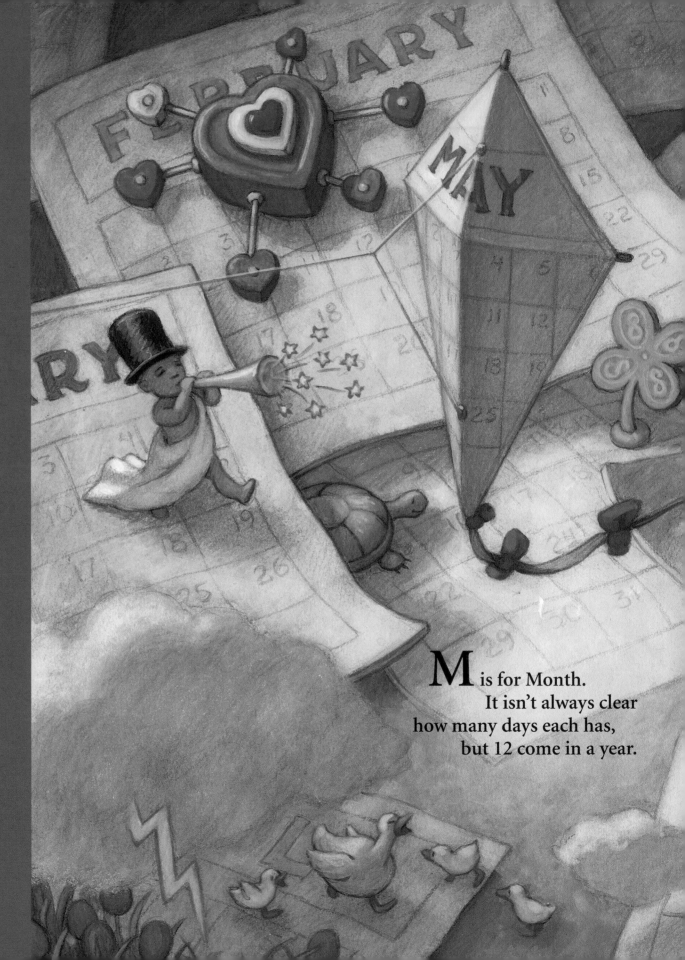

M is for Month.
It isn't always clear
how many days each has,
but 12 come in a year.

M
m

N n

N is for the Night sky.
Looking up so far,
we can figure out the time
by the position of the stars.

Early astronomers determined time at night by using a tool called a merkhet. A merkhet lined up with the North Star creating an imaginary line to the earth called a meridian. The astronomers watched and made notes of when certain stars crossed the meridian to calculate the time. It is one of the world's oldest astronomy tools and was developed in Egypt around 600 BC.

The astrolabe is another ancient tool that was used to tell time. It is flat and round with a map of the universe on the front with the North Star at the center. It was used to calculate the time of sunrise or sunset. Some cultures still use astrolabes to determine the time of sunrise and sunset. One of the largest collections of astrolabes is in Chicago's Adler Planetarium.

An observatory is a place to watch and record the moon, planets, and stars. It also is a place where astronomers study the weather and keep track of time. Observatories have been used since ancient times all over the world.

The first observatory in the United States was the Naval Observatory. It is located in Washington, D.C. Before accurate time was easily available, the Naval Observatory and other observatories around the world used balls each day to show the noon hour. These balls, called time balls, were mounted on a pole high on top of the observatory. Exactly at noon, the time ball would slide down the pole. Anyone who wanted to know the exact noon hour watched for the dropping time ball. This was especially helpful for sailors in ships heading out to sea. Today, the United States Naval Observatory is our country's official timekeeper.

O o

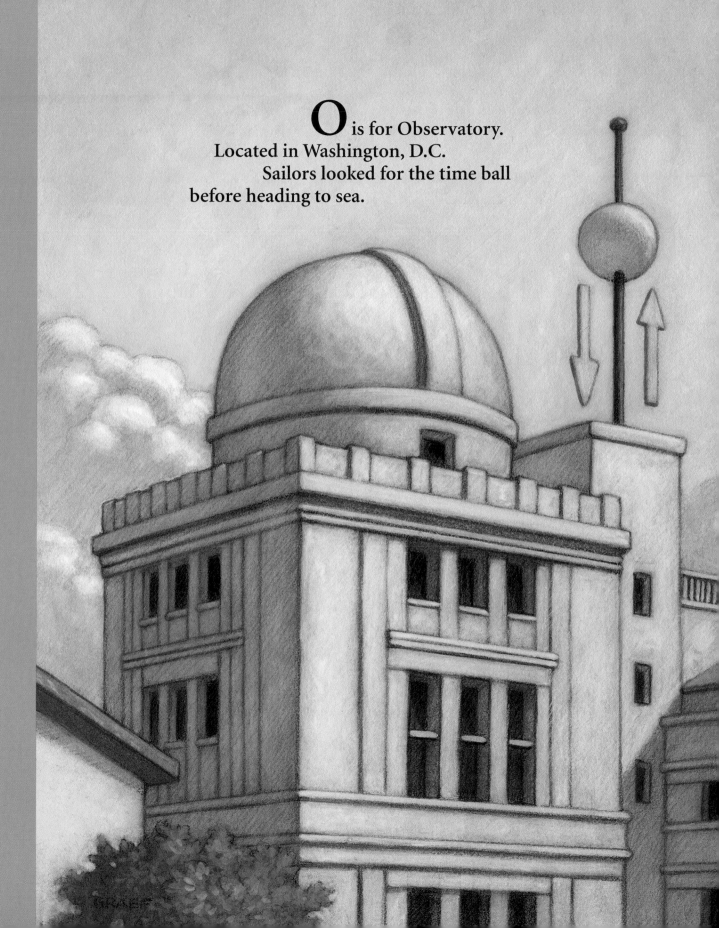

O is for Observatory.
Located in Washington, D.C.
Sailors looked for the time ball
before heading to sea.

P is for Pendulum,
> watch it swing.
Power for a clock,
> a weight tied to a string.

Galileo Galilei was a scientist, mathematician, and astronomer. In 1583 while sitting in the Cathedral of Pisa, he looked up at the ceiling and noticed the lamps swaying back and forth. Galilei timed their speed by counting his pulse. He decided that a swinging weight, called a pendulum, takes the same amount of time going backward or forward no matter what its size. The length of the rope or string is what makes the difference.

Galilei thought he could use a pendulum to move the gears of a clock. He made a drawing of a clock powered by a pendulum but never built one to test his theory.

It wasn't until 1656 that Dutch scientist Christiaan Huygens built the first pendulum clock. The pendulum increased the accuracy of clocks and was one of the most important changes in clock history until the invention of the quartz clock 271 years later.

Pp

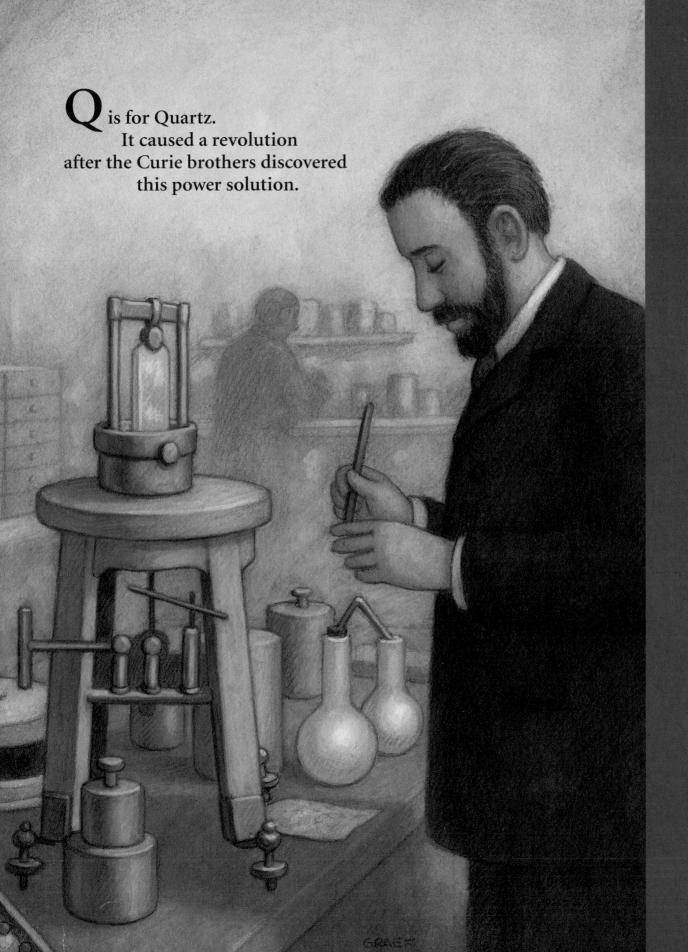

Q is for Quartz.
It caused a revolution
after the Curie brothers discovered
this power solution.

In 1880, French brothers and scientists Jacques and Pierre Curie discovered that certain materials vibrate and produce an electric charge when pressure is applied to them. Quartz is one of the most abundant minerals on the earth and has this ability.

Warren Marrison worked at the Bell Telephone Laboratory. In 1927 he used the Curie brothers' discovery along with other scientific discoveries to make the first quartz clock. Quartz crystals replaced the pendulum, giving clocks the power needed to keep time. Quartz clocks were much more accurate in keeping time than previous timepieces. This invention changed the way most clocks and watches were made. It created what is called the quartz revolution in clockmaking.

R r

R is for the Railroad Companies
that took up the lead,
setting a standard time—
but not everyone agreed.

Before the United States had a time that was the same for everyone, called a standard time, a train's arrival or departure schedule was based on its own local time. Travelers weren't sure when to go to a station to catch a train or when to pick someone up from an arriving train.

The railroad companies didn't like this confusion about time and travel. They decided to divide the country into time zones and make time the same in each zone. Not everyone used trains on a regular basis. Many people and towns did not like giving up their local time for the convenience of the railroads and its passengers. The federal government agreed with the railroads and a standard time was made law in 1918.

The United States is so large, it was divided into four time zones: eastern standard time, central standard time, mountain standard time, and Pacific standard time. Later, most of Alaska became Alaska standard time. Hawaii and a part of Alaska became Hawaii-Aleutian time.

S is for Shadow.
A stick in the sand
used to mark time
as shadows crossed the land.

S s

In ancient times, a simple stick stuck in the ground may have been the first way to measure the passage of time. These are known as shadow clocks. As the sun moves across the sky, shadow lengths change. They become shorter at noon and longer toward evening. Obelisks, four-sided pillars ending in a point on the top built by ancient Egyptians, were also shadow clocks.

Sundials are a more accurate version of the shadow clock.

A timepiece is an instrument to measure the passage of time. Simple timepieces like shadow clocks and sundials of long ago were available to anyone. Some were made with expensive materials by skilled craftspeople for emperors, kings, and queens. In many cultures, incense, oil, candles, and water were used to mark the passage of time. As timepieces became more complicated with moving parts, they became more expensive to make. Not many people could afford them.

German clockmaker Peter Henlein is considered to be the first maker of portable clocks and watches. He started making watches around 1505. The first watch worn on a woman's wrist was made in 1868. It was called a wristlet. During World War I, soldiers started using a leather strap to keep pocket watches on their wrists so their hands would be free for using weapons. Men have worn wristwatches ever since.

T is for Timepiece.
All kinds of devices
over the centuries—
many sizes and prices.

T t

The most accurate timepieces today are atomic clocks. They are powered by atoms. Today, many people depend on cell phones for time. Cell phones receive their time from atomic clocks.

Clocks and watches today are inexpensively mass-produced. Most households have a clock, and wristwatches are seen on people of all ages and social backgrounds.

U is for Units.
How to measure
time going by
during work or pleasure.

The ancient Romans divided days into two parts: ante meridiem (a.m.), which is Latin for before midday, and post meridiem (p.m.), which means after midday. As timepieces became more advanced, smaller units of measurement were added. First came an hour, then a minute, and then a second: 60 seconds make up 1 minute, 60 minutes make up 1 hour, and 24 hours make up 1 day.

Some units of time are so small they aren't displayed on clocks. Special stopwatches that do keep track of these smaller units are used during the Olympics and other athletic races. Winners and losers are sometimes separated by as little as 1/100 of a second. That is one second divided by 100. Small units of time matter.

U u

Foliot

Weight

Verge

Pallets

Barrel

Weight

V is for Verge Escapement
inside of a clock;
hear when it moves
ticktock, ticktock.

GRAEF

V
V

The most important invention in early mechanical clocks was the verge escapement, also known as the crown wheel escapement. No one knows for sure who invented it but it was probably added to timepieces around the thirteenth century. It has three main parts: the crown wheel, the verge with pallets on each end, and the foliot with adjustable weights. The movement of these parts causes the pallets on the verge to hit the crown wheel, which makes the ticktock sound of a clock.

This timekeeping invention, although a huge improvement, could lose or gain 30 minutes or more a day. This is not very accurate by today's standards, but back then it was impressive.

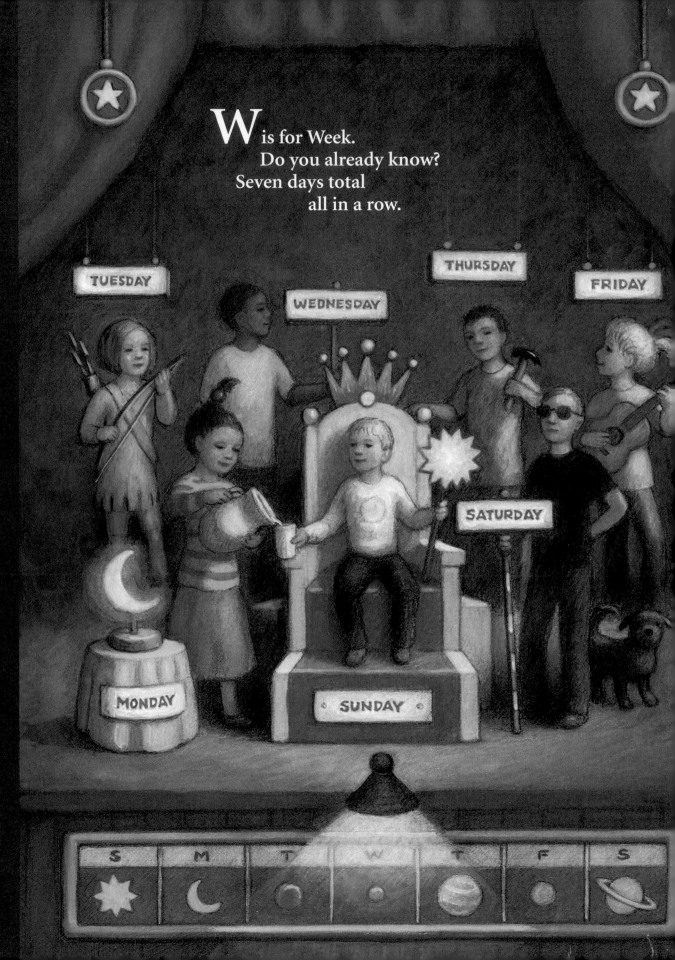

W is for Week.
Do you already know?
Seven days total
all in a row.

A week has been seven days since recorded history. The calendar we use today is based on the Roman calendar that used a seven-day week. Sunday was named for the sun, Monday for the moon. Planets and Roman gods were used for the rest of the week: Tuesday for Mars, Wednesday for Mercury, Thursday for Jupiter, Friday for Venus, and Saturday for Saturn.

When the Anglo-Saxons invaded Britain around AD 450, they started using this Roman calendar. They changed some names of the week to honor their gods. We still use these names today. Tuesday was named after Tiw, god of war and justice. Wednesday was named after their most powerful god, Woden. Thursday was named after Thor, known for his powerful hammer. Friday was named after the goddess Frigg, Woden's wife.

The use of Roman numerals started around 500 BC and lasted throughout Europe for nearly 1,800 years. Clockmakers and watchmakers still use Roman numerals on their face designs because of the classic style and elegant look. In Waterbury, Connecticut, there is a 245-foot-tall clock tower with four sides. Roman numerals five feet tall are used on all four sides of the clock faces.

Clocks don't always use numbers to display the time. The Allen-Bradley clock, in Milwaukee, Wisconsin, is one of the largest four-faced clocks in the world. It uses triangle shapes for each hour.

Clocks that use hands to show time are called analog clocks. Some clocks don't have hands and use only numbers like those on a microwave oven or computer. These clocks are called digital clocks. Military clocks use a 24-hour clock. The dial starts with 00:01 for one minute after midnight and continues to 24:00 for midnight.

X is for the number 10 painted on a clock's dial.
Done in Roman numerals—
it's an ancient style.

Y is for a Year.
People stay up late
to welcome in the New Year—
it's time to celebrate.

NEXT YEAR

NOW

JANUARY
①

Yy

The New Year celebration is one of the oldest holidays, dating back over 4,000 years. Our New Year starts on January 1. On New Year's Eve parties are held to say good-bye to the old year and to welcome in the New Year at midnight.

Not all countries celebrate the New Year on January 1. Some countries and religions use different calendars. The Jewish New Year is called Rosh Hashanah. It is a two-day celebration. The dates change based on the Jewish lunar calendar.

The Chinese New Year, called *Yuan Tan*, begins between mid-January and mid-February, depending on the Chinese lunar calendar. The celebration lasts 15 days. It ends with lanterns of many sizes and shapes hanging in the streets and carried by children. The lanterns are usually red, symbolizing good fortune.

Z z

The earth is divided into 24 different time zones. Each time zone has 15 lines, or degrees, of longitude starting with the prime meridian in Greenwich, England. Each time zone is given a letter of the alphabet. Each letter is assigned a code word according to a phonetic alphabet. This alphabet code is called Zulu time. The code makes it easier to understand exactly what time it is when communicating or traveling around the world. Zulu time is also called Universal Time Coordinate, UTC for short. Zulu time uses a 24-hour military clock. It is used in plane and ship navigation, radio communications, weather reports, and by militaries.

The letter Z or Zulu refers to the prime meridian at Greenwich, England. Crossing the United States starting at the East Coast and ending in Hawaii, the time zones you would travel through would be Romeo, Sierra, Tango, Uniform, Victor, and Whiskey.

Zulu time is the end of our alphabet of time. We all depend on the accuracy of our timepieces. Horologists and scientists around the world continue to work on ways to improve how we measure time.

Z is for Zulu time.
This keeps an order
of what time it is
across all borders.

Marie and Roland Smith

Award-winning author Roland Smith and his wife and fellow author, Marie Smith, have collaborated on numerous titles, including *S is for Smithsonian: America's Museum Alphabet*, *W is for Waves: An Ocean Alphabet*, and *Z is for Zookeeper: A Zoo Alphabet*. Marie and Roland grew up in Oregon and now live on a small farm south of Portland. Roland is the author of many books for children, including *Chupacabra*, *Cryptid Hunters*, *Tentacles*, *Zach's Lie*, the Storm Runners series, and *The Captain's Dog: My Journey with the Lewis and Clark Tribe*, which won the Pacific Northwest Booksellers Award. He has also penned Sleeping Bear Press's middle-grade series, I, Q.

Renée Graef

Renée Graef has illustrated more than 70 books for children, including *What's Looking at You, Kid?* and *D is for Dala Horse: A Nordic Countries Alphabet* with Sleeping Bear Press; the Kirsten books in the American Girl Collection; and many of the My First Little House books by Laura Ingalls Wilder. Renée lives in Milwaukee, Wisconsin, and Los Angeles, California. Learn more about Renée and her work at www.reneegraef.com.